Thomas Gisborne

Walks in a Forest

Poems Descriptive of Scenery and Incidents Characteristic of a Forest at Different Seasons of the Year

Thomas Gisborne

Walks in a Forest
Poems Descriptive of Scenery and Incidents Characteristic of a Forest at Different Seasons of the Year

ISBN/EAN: 9783337811563

Printed in Europe, USA, Canada, Australia, Japan

Cover: Foto ©Thomas Meinert / pixelio.de

More available books at **www.hansebooks.com**

WALKS

IN A

FOREST.

OR,

POEMS

DESCRIPTIVE OF SCENERY AND INCIDENTS CHARACTERISTIC OF

A FOREST,

AT DIFFERENT SEASONS OF THE YEAR

INSCRIBED TO THE

REVEREND WILLIAM MASON,

OF ASTON, IN YORKSHIRE.

LONDON:

PRINTED BY J. DAVIS,

FOR B. AND J. WHITE, FLEET-STREET.

MDCCXCIV.

TO THE

REVEREND WILLIAM MASON.

MY DEAR SIR,

  THOUGH you are unapprized of the exist ence of the following trifles, you will easily discove whence they come; and I am confident, from the proof which I have already experienced of your partial kind ness, that you will accept them favourably. However lit tle gratification they may be able to afford you as poetry you will be pleased with them as a tribute of friendship They are meant to delineate the scenes and incidents which they notice, with particularity sufficient to mark the characteristic features of each; and to avoid, on the one hand, vague and indeterminate description; and on the other, such a degree of detail as would prove scarcely
            intelligible

DEDICATION.

intelligible to perfons not accuſtomed ſtudiouſly to contemplate the face of nature, and might appear tedious and minute even to accurate obſervers. The woodland tracts which gave riſe to them have been admired by us together. To myſelf they have been familiar from my childhood. And long familiarity at length produced the ſketches now inſcribed to you in the intervals of thoſe hours, which you know to have been much occupied with more ſerious purſuits.

I am, dear Sir,

Your obliged and affectionate friend,

THE AUTHOR.

CONTENTS.

	Page
WALK THE FIRST. SPRING	1
WALK THE SECOND. SUMMER—NOON	11
WALK THE THIRD. SUMMER—MOONLIGHT	19
WALK THE FOURTH. AUTUMN	27
WALK THE FIFTH. WINTER—SNOW	37
WALK THE SIXTH. WINTER—FROST	43

WALKS IN A FOREST.

WALK THE FIRST.

SPRING.

" THE meanest * herb we trample in the field,
" Or nurture in the garden, when its leaf
" At Winter's touch is blasted, and its place
" Forgotten, soon its vernal buds renews,
" And from short slumber wakes to life again.
" Man wakes no more! Man, valiant, glorious, wise,

---

* Αι, αι, ται μαλακαι μεν επαν κατα καπον ολωνται,
Η τα χλωρα σελινα, το τ' ευθαλες κλον ανηθον,
Υστερον αυ ζωονται, και εις ετος αλλο φυονται.
Αμμες δ' οι μεγαλοι, και καρτεροι, η σοφοι ανδρες,
Οπποτε πρωτα θανωμες, ανακοοι εν χθονι κοιλα
Ευδομες ευ μαλα μακρον, ατερμονα, νηγρετον υπνον.

MOSCHUS, IN EPITAPH. BION.

" When

" When death once chills him sinks in sleep profound,
" A long, unconscious, never ending sleep!"
So mourn'd the untutor'd bard, wandering when May,
As now, the plains revived; ere * sprang the Prince
Of righteousness, with healing on his wings,
Triumphant from the sepulchre; while he,
Hell's Ruler, he who late, madden'd with joy,
Had pointed to his Powers in air convened,
With many a scoff and many a bitter sneer
Impious, the sad procession as it moved
From Calvary to the yet unclosed tomb,
View'd the grave yield its conqueror; and aghast,
And from his eminence as by lightning hurl'd,
Shunn'd in the deepest midnight of his realms
The wrath of earth and heaven's Almighty Lord.
Said the complaining lay, " Man wakes no more?"
O blind, who read'st not in the teeming soil,
The freshening meadow, and the bursting wood,
A nobler lesson! God, who in the gloom
Of Gentile darkness on an erring world
Pitying look'd down, nor without † witness left
His providential care, bade Nature's voice

* Moschus flourished about two hundred years before the Christian era.
† Acts xiv. 17. Romans i. 20.

To man his future destiny suggest:
Bade Spring with annual admonition hold
Her emblematic taper; not with blaze
Potent each shade of doubt and fear to chase,
Yet friendly through the perilous dusk to aid
His steps, till the dawn crimson'd, and arose
The long expected day-star in the East.
    That star has risen; and with a light, which shames
The sun's meridian splendor, has illumed
The distant wonders of eternity.
Yet may this sylvan wild, from Winter's grasp
Now rescued, to the musing mind recall
Its promised immortality; while roves
The eye unsated with delight from shade
To shade, from grove to thicket, from near groupes
To yon primæval woods with darkening sweep
Retiring; and with beauty sees the whole
Kindle, and glow with renovated life.
Each native of the forest, from the rude
And towering trunk down to the tangled bush,
Its own peculiar character resumes.
Chief of the glade, the oak its foliage stain'd
With tender olive and pale brown protrudes,
Proud of a shelter'd monarch, proud to lend

A chaplet still to British loyalty.
Even yet with ruddy spoils from Autumn won
Loaded, the beech its lengthen'd buds untwines.
Its knotted bloom secured, the ash puts forth
The tardy leaf: the hawthorn wraps its boughs
In snowy mantle: from the vivid greens
That shine around, the holly, winter's pride,
Recedes abash'd. The willow, in yon vale,
Its silver lining to the breeze upturns,
And rustling aspens shiver by the brook;
While the unsullied stream, from April showers
Refined, each sparkling pebble shews that decks
Its bottom; and each scaly habitant
Quick glancing in the shallows, or in 'quest
Of plunder slowly sailing in the deep.
Beneath the shadowing canopy the ground
Glitters with flowery dies; the primrose, first
In mossy dell returning Spring to greet;
Pilewort, with varnish'd bloom, and spotted leaf;
And hooded arum, with its purple club;
Anemone*, now robed in virgin white,
Now blushing with faint crimson; changeful spurge †,

* Wood anemone. Anemone nemorosa Linn.
† Wood spurge. Euphorbia amygdaloides Linn.

On

On redden'd ſtem turgid with milky ſap,
And circled with dark foliage, rearing high
Its golden head; ſorrel [*], whoſe modeſt cups
Midſt verdure wan their ſtreaky veins conceal;
The pendent harebell; and the ſcentleſs plant [†],
That with the violet's borrow'd form and hue
The unſkilful wanderer in the ſhade deceives.
Flutter with wings the branches, and reſound
With notes that ſuit a foreſt. Hoarſely ſcreams
The jay. With ſhrill and oft repeated cry
Her angular courſe, alternate riſe and fall,
The woodpecker purſues; then to the trunk
Cloſe clinging, with inceſſant knockings ſhakes
The hollow bark; through every cell the ſtroke
Echoes; hope gliſtens on her verdant plumes,
And brighter ſcarlet ſparkles on her creſt.
Chatters the reſtleſs pie. In ſober brown
Dreſt, but with nature's tendereſt pencil touch'd,
The wryneck her monotonous complaint
Continues [‡]; harbinger of her, who doom'd

---

[*] Wood ſorrel. Oxalis acetoſa Linn.   [†] Dog's violet. Viola canina Linn.

[‡] The Welſh conſider this bird as the forerunner or ſervant of the cuckoo, and call it gwâs y gog, or the cuckoo's attendant. The Swedes regard it in the ſame light. Pennant's Brit. Zool. 4th edit. vol. i. p. 238. In the midland counties of England the common people call it the cuckoo's maiden.

Never

Never the sympathetic joy to know
That warms the mother cowering o'er her young,
Some stranger robs, and to that stranger's love
Her egg commits unnatural; the nurse
Deluded the voracious nestling feeds
With toil unceasing, and amazed beholds
Its form gigantic and discordant hue.
Meanwhile the tuneful race their brooding mates
Cheer, perch'd at hand; or with parental care
From twig to twig their timid offspring lead;
Teach them to seize the unwary gnat, to poise
Their pinions, in short flights their strength to prove,
And venturous trust the bosom of the air.

 Nor want these lawns that terminate the woods
Their tenants. O'er the gorse with agile bounds
Spring the light deer, and sportive scour the plain
In mock pursuit. Pour'd from the neighbouring farms
Wide stray the cattle. Mark yon wearied herd;
Mark the unguarded front, the slender limb,
The tawny ear, and sable-vested side.
From Scotia's hills they come, there wont to pick
From rocky chinks the blade, or bruise the tops
Of heath and prickly furze, when winter reign'd;
Or in the stormy Hebrides forlorn

Rush duly from the moor, scenting afar [*]
The ebbing tide, and prowling on the sand,
And midst the slippery stones, with weeds marine
And ocean's refuse famine's rage repel.
Now in mild clime and copious pasture placed
Their driver quits them; he, who deck'd in plaid,
And plumed bonnet, had their steps pursued
All the long tedious march; and still when beat
The shower, around his limbs regardless wrapt
His chequer'd covering; and when cross'd the road
Some spring's pure current, from the knapsack drew
His bowl and oaten flour, and frugal mix'd
His fare, delicious to his palate braced
By labour, and by luxury unpall'd.

    Tremble the glades. Yon hill's majestic gloom
Portentous shakes. Heard ye not Britain's voice
Speaking in thunder to the woods? She calls
Their long protected growth her shores to guard
With tributary aid, and round her isle
Found on the seas an adamantine wall.
Pierce we those shades. The solitude resounds
With busy life. The uplifted axe, urged deep
By sinewy arms, while the well planted feet

[*] See Pennant's Tour in Scotland.

Keep firm the muscles of the straining back,
Delves the resisting trunk; from every stroke
Wide fly the fragments. With impetuous force,
While from his furious sweep the victors fly,
Prone falls the sylvan monarch; with the dread
Concussion quakes the forest; loudly crash
His splinter'd arms, and ruin spreads the ground.
Now this now that way drawn the harsh saw grates,
Severing the mighty limbs. Those strip the bark;
In heaps these rear it. Those the thinner boughs
Hew to fit lengths; these in well order'd tiers
Dispose them, sedulous the pile to raise,
Which, with stout greensward roof from wet secured,
May burn to sooty charcoal. Near its side
Yon children in the ground their pliant poles
Fix, and the tops unite: these, interlaced
With twigs, his wigwam as the Indian weaves
In transatlantic wilds, or cloth'd with turf
As builds his summer hut on mountain top
The Cambrian herdsman, shelter shall afford,
While the slow-kindled mass they tend, and watch
To ope in time fresh inlets for the breeze,
And pierce new chimnies for the imprison'd smoke.
Soon the peel'd trunk, reft of its branched head,

And

And by mechanic force upheaved, shall quit
Its native lawn, while the tired oxen pant,
And groans the wain beneath the ponderous load.

 So fade the chieftains of the wood; their place
Knows them no more; the desolated blank
Gapes, and admits the long excluded day.
Yet swiftly through the void their shoots shall push
Contiguous saplings, and with stately stems
And ample spread shall emulate their sires.
Thus when the statesman and the warrior fall,
Britain dejected mourns; but soon a race,
With memory of paternal virtue warm'd,
Pleads in the senate, conquers in the field;
And while approving heaven the purpose crowns,
Upholds the reign of freedom, and of law,
Of social order, and domestic peace.

WALK THE SECOND.

SUMMER.——NOON.

THE solstice rages; Nature sinks opprest
Beneath the sultry glow. Hide me, ye woods,
Hide in your shades impenetrable; waft
A breeze reviving from your inmost depths;
While your tall trunks between I gaze abroad
On the parch'd world, or watch the trooping deer
Safe in the covert from the scorching ray
Shelter'd. They fly not me; no murderous tube
Gleams in my hand: but far aloof they shun
Him, whose green vesture and suspicious gait
Mark him their authorised destroyer. Few
And those short-seeming hours since morn have past;
Yet this brief interval the clime has changed
From temperate zone to torrid. Scatter'd clouds,
With orient blush empurpled, half obscured
The rising orb of light; gray mists diffused

O'er the wide lawn, and from the wooded hill
Dim through their skirts discerned retiring flow,
His struggling beams restrain'd; yon reverend oaks,
Fronting the east, across the ample vale
Stretch'd their long shadows; glisten'd bright with dew
The grass; and cool and balmy breathed the air.
Now from the burning firmament the Sun
Each cloud has driven; with universal light
Blazing, the earth repels the dazzled eye,
Save where a lonely spot of shade lies close
Beneath some massy tree, or woods extend
Their dark recesses; the faint traveller's step
The tann'd and slippery plain deceives; and fierce
As when in Indian realms it rages, heat
The breeze-deserted atmosphere inflames.

 Yet cannot heat's meridian rage deter
The cottage-matron from her annual toil.
On that rough bank behold her, bent to reap
The full-grown fern, her harvest, and prepare
Her balls of purifying ashes. First
A firm bare spot she chooses for the hearth;
Then strikes the steel, the tinder covers light
With wither'd leaves and dry; then stoops to fan
The glimmering sparks, and motionless remains,

Watching the infant flame from side to side
Run through the thin materials. Round her stray
Children or grandchildren, a cheerful train,
Dispersed among the bushes; earnest each
To execute the task her voice assigns,
Half sport, half labour, fit for early youth.
One plies the hook, the rake another trails;
Another, staggering, bears the verdant load
Uplifted in his arms; another hastes
Her apron's burthen to discharge. The dame
Receives their tribute; part she heaps aside
In store for night, the embers to preserve
From quenching dews; part on the kindled pile
Cautious she sprinkles, duly with her fork
Raising the half-burnt strata to admit
Supply of flame-supporting air; as oft,
The enliven'd mass glows bright, and crackles loud.
Issuing from frequent chinks the smoke pours forth
Its curling volumes; not as when condensed
By evening's gelid atmosphere, it creeps
Below the hill, and draws along the plain
Its lengthen'd line, and dies away diffused
In hazy vapour; but aspiring towers
(For not a breath the aerial ocean moves)

In

In column perpendicular, far seen
With broad and dusky head; to pilgrim's eye
As view'd o'er Salem's plain the palm ascends.
Hence shall the housewife in the distant town
With eager gaze her whiten'd cloth admire,
And flight the produce of Hibernian looms.

 Oft from these fires pernicious sparks adrift
Borne by the wind; or thrown by rustic hands
With secret purpose that the soil, from base
And noxious vegetation freed, may yield
Salubrious pasture to the grazing herd;
Seize the dead grass, the furzy brake invade,
Kindle the matted brushwood, and from hill
To hill the sudden conflagration spread.
Woe to the solitary oak that meets
The fiery deluge in its course; the blaze
Round the roots rattles, climbs the singed trunk,
Devours the leaves, and o'er the topmost boughs
Its smoke-stain'd canopy triumphant rears.
Roused by the unaccustom'd sound the fox
Starts from his rest, the scent of flame inhales
Dismayed, and rushes forth; the heath-cock wakes,
And springs in terror through the fervid air.
Meanwhile the clouds dark rising from the spoil

The neighbouring hamlets, confcious of the caufe,
View unalarm'd: but at the clofe of day
The horizon red with fettled glow, and oft
With fpiry flafhes gleaming, fills with awe
Tracts far remote; and to the boding mind
The picture holds of harvefts ftored in vain,
Of ravaged farms, and villages deftroy'd.

 Mark how yon pool, by unexhaufted fprings
Still nurtured, draws the multitudes that graze
The plains adjacent. On the bank worn bare,
And printed with ten thoufand fteps, the colts
In fhifting groupes combine; or to the brink
Defcending, dip their pafterns in the wave.
Bolder the horned tribes, or lefs of heat
And teafing infects patient, far from fhore
Bathe deep their chefts; or by thick fwarms purfued,
Lafh their tormented fides, and ftamping quick
And oft, the muddy fluid fcatter round.
Fix'd many an hour, till milder fkies recall
Defire of long forgotten food, they ftand
Each in its place; fave when fome wearied beaft
The preffure of the crowd no longer brooks,
Or in mere vagrant mood its ftation quits
Reftlefs; or fome intruder, from afar

           Flying

Flying o'er hill and plain the gadbee's fting,
(For ftill the dreaded hum fhe hears, and fhakes
The air with iterated lowings), fpies
The watry gleam. With wildly-toffing head,
And tail projected far, and maddening gait,
She plunges in, and breaks the ranks, and fpreads
Confufion, till conftrain'd at length fhe ftops,
Wedged in the throng. Beneath a neighbouring bufh,
Poor fhelter from the potent ray, reclines
The ruftic boy to count his mafter's herd
Sent from yon hamlet; left fome ftraggler, feized
By fharp and fudden malady, fhould pine
Untended in the wood; or refolute
To crop forbidden pafture, overleap
The well-plafh'd fence, and roam through diftant fields.
Panting, bareheaded, and with outftretch'd arms
He fleeps; and dreams of winter's frofty gale,
Of funlefs thickets, breeze-attracting ftreams,
Morn's dewy frefhnefs, and cool reft at eve.
  From the whole furface of the tepid earth,
But moft from rivers rippling fwift, and pools,
And trickling fprings, and oozy fwamps exhaled,
A vapoury fteam floats, with the loaded air
Yet uncombined; and undulating ftill

And

And ever twinkling, o'er the diſtant woods
Sheds a blue haze, and dims their ſhadowy forms.
Where through the tufted coverts of the grove
Deſcends that opening glade, leading the eye
To ſcenes beyond the foreſt's bounds removed,
How nobly midſt the fading objects ſtands
Yon* fane pre-eminent! It warms my heart,
When through the wide-ſpread provinces I ſtray
Of this fair realm, to view the ſlender ſpire
And maſſy tower from deep-embowering ſhades
Oft riſing in the vale, or on the ſrde
Of gently-ſloping hills, or loftier placed,
Crowning the wooded eminence. It looks
As though we own'd a God, adored his power,
Revered his wiſdom, loved his mercy; deem d.
He claims the empire of this lower world,
And marks the deeds of its inhabitants.
It looks as though we deem'd he fills all ſpace
Preſent throughout; and ſits on heaven's high throne
With ears attentive to the poor man's prayer.
It looks as though we ſhrunk not from the thought.
Of that laſt manſion (laſt, as far as earth
Detains us), where in ſolemn ſilence laid.

* Lichfield Cathedral.

D Our

Our duſt ſhall ſlumber; till a voice, like that
Which ſpeaking by the aſtoniſhed* prophet's mouth,
Rouſed the dry bones that ſtrew'd the ſpacious vale
To ſudden life, ſhall call the unnumber'd dead
Primæval Adam with his lateſt ſons,
From every clime before their judge's face
To ſtand, and hear their everlaſting doom.

   God clothes his works with beauty. What tho' here
He has not wrapp'd in clouds the mountain's head
Magnificent, nor piled the fractured rock;
Nor delved the ſtony cavern ſtretching wide
Its unſupported roof; nor down the ſteep
Pour'd the rude cataract; nor bid the lake
Expand its ſplendid mirror to the ſun;
Nor ocean's billowy ſurges waſh the baſe
Of promontories, whoſe white cliffs with fowl
Swarming of every ſeaborn tribe, reſound
With countleſs wings, and never wearied cries:
Yet has his hand the intermingling charms
Of hill and valley, lawn, and winding dell,
In rich exuberance ſpread; yet has his hand
Hung theſe wild banks with ſylvan majeſty.

        * Ezekiel, chap. xxxvii.

WALK THE THIRD.

SUMMER.——MOONLIGHT.

THE glow of eve is faded. Scarce the Weſt
Retains a pale memorial of the beams
Which fired it, when the horizontal clouds,
With purple dies and fiſſures edged with gold,
Streak'd the calm ether; while the hills were veil'd
In glimmering haze, more tender as their chain
Approach'd the fount of brightneſs, fainter ſtill
Where ſunk the parting orb, and with the ſky
In undiſtinguiſhable ſplendor join'd.
Frown'd the dark oak, and with contraſting gloom
Athwart the blaze its ſable ſhadows flung.
Soon o'er the hill the yellow-tinctured moon
Roſe through the twilight, and with ſlanting ray
Gilded the topmoſt boughs; while all the vale
And all its ſloping boundaries lay wrapt
In ſhade unvaried. Now with leſſening ſphere

And filver afpect climbing, through the leaves
And thinner fpray a tremulous gleam fhe throws,
Chequering the mofly path beneath our feet.
Round her the ftars and planetary balls
With cloudlefs luftre burn; not ranged in heaven
With mere defign a twinkling aid to lend
To the late-wandering ftranger, nor ordain'd
To rule our deftinies, as craft averr'd,
And antient ignorance believed, thy power,
Parent of all, they fpeak: they tell of worlds
Innumerable, warm'd by other funs,
And peopled with innumerable hofts
Of beings, wondrous all, nor lefs than man
Work of thy hands, and children of thy care!

 While with their heads beneath their ruffled plumes
Conceal'd, the birds that fported during day,
Reft in thefe fheltering bufhes, at whofe roots
The vivid worm its nightly fpark illumes;
And couching in that brake the timorous deer
Slumbers forgetful of each paft alarm;
Iffue from every lurking place the tribes
That animate the dufk. Heard ye the owl
Hoot to her mate refponfive? 'Twas not fhe
Whom floating on white pinions near his barn

The farmer views well pleafed, and bids his boy
Forbear her neft; but fhe who cloth'd in robe
Of unobtrufive hue, preys not befide
Moufe-haunted cornftacks, and the threfher's floor,
But prowls for plunder in the lonely wood.
Hark, from the quivering bough its whirring note,
Loud as the noife of bufy maiden's wheel,
The foe nocturnal of the infect train,
Mifnamed the goatfucker, prolongs *; then flies
With beak expanded wide, and throat enlarged
Even to its utmoft ftretch, its cuftom'd food
Swallowing voracious. In uncertain jerks
Flitting, and twittering fhrill and weak, the bat
Joins in the chafe. Nor is the chafe in vain.
For ever and anon the beetle dull

---

* " This bird agrees with the fwallow tribe in food and in the manner of taking it; differs in the time of preying, flying only by night; fo with fome juftice may be called a nocturnal fwallow. Scopoli feems to credit the report of its fucking the teats of goats; an error delivered down from the days of Ariftotle. Its notes are moft fingular; the loudeft fo much refembles that of a large fpinning-wheel, that the Welch call this bird aderyn y droell, or the wheel-bird. It begins its fong moft punctually on the clofe of day; fitting ufually on a bare bough. The noife is fo very violent, as to give a fenfible vibration to any little building it chances to alight on, and emit this fpecies of note." Pennant's Britifh Zoology, vol. i. p. 416, 417.

Smites

Smites us with sudden stroke, stopping at once
Its heavy hum; while moths of size and form
And motion various flutter by, with plumes
Less gorgeous, not less delicate, than theirs
Whose painted wings the noontide flowers adorn.
Now from the hollow trunk, its den, leaps forth
The tawny wild-cat, fiercest of the beasts
That roam in Britain's forests; wont on high
To seize the rapid squirrel, or by guile
Pluck from its nest the unsuspecting dove,
Or to the ground descending thin the race
That bores the sandy warren. Creeping slow
The weasel, and in silence, through the fern
Steals on the dozing leveret. From her seat
She starts, and bears away the assailant fix'd
Fast to her neck, and from the flowing vein
Sucking the vital current. Lo, she falls.
The puny murderer slinks into the brake
From the drain'd carcass, sated with the blood.

Why rush'd that horseman with impetuous course
Across the glade, still looking back; while shook
The forest with the deep-toned bloodhound's roar?
I know his deeds. Ere long on yonder plain
Again shall we behold him; though he strives

His chafers to miflead, and round thofe banks
Artful his circuit takes, there will he feek
The outlet of the wild. This day at noon
With ftaff and halter in his hand he ftray'd
As watchful of the grazing tribes; and feem'd
An herdfman bent his wandering colt to find,
And from the fcanty common lead him home
To more abundant pafture. Other thoughts
Lay lurking in his breaft. From prying gaze
Within the hollow lining of his coat
Cover'd, the mufket by malignant art
For depredation form'd, in feparate lengths
Disjointed, as mufician parts his flute,
He bore. With never-erring fkill, matured
By long experience, in the numerous crowd
The well-fed buck he mark'd, fingling at once
His deftined victim, as the fragrant herb
He cropp'd, unconfcious of impending fate.
Perch'd on the fummit of the blafted oak
The raven eyed him (often had fhe traced
His purpofe), and in filence ominous
Waited her offal portion of the prey.
Meanwhile, a fhot delufive, in the woods

At

At diftance due by fly confederate fired,
Alarm'd the keeper's ear. Inftant he urged
From glade to glade the vain purfuit, and left
The endanger'd fpot unguarded. The fafe hour
The plunderer feized; the tube with fpeed reftored
To native fhape he charged, levell'd his aim,
And drew the trigger. Clang'd the fteel, and flafh'd
Deftruction. Swift he dragg'd the bleeding fpoil,
And plung'd the quivering limbs and branched creft
Deep in the brake, and fled. Bold he return'd
When twilight lent to guilt her dubious veil
At eve, prepared his booty to convey
To diftant mart, where pamper'd luxury
With indifcriminate rage her dainties buys,
Regardlefs whence they come, or how procured.
But roufed by fudden tramplings, ere the load
Was pack'd, acrofs his fteed the deer he throws,
And mounts in hafte. For now their nightly rounds
The keepers hold; and foon the ranging dogs
Sagacious note the deed, and touch the place
Of flaughter. With loud roar they tell the tale;
And over hill and lawn fcenting the blood,
By jolting agitation liquefied,

At

At intervals ſtill dropping from the wound,
Through all his bends the frighted robber chafe.
Mark where they come: eager behind them ſweep
Their maſters. From our fight lo all are loſt,
Purſuers and purſued. Croſs we this knoll,
And meet them as they circle round the ſkirts
Of that impenetrable wood. There flies
The caitiff! Nearer and ſtill nearer borne
Hang on his ſteps his foes. And now his form
Shouting they recognize, and fiercer drive
Their ſteeds. For long ſuſpicious had they gueſs'd
His ſecret wiles; and oft at dead of night
His cottage had they ſought, and arm'd with force
Of legal claims and juſt authority,
Entrance demanded, and with patient toil
Explored each dark receſs, anxious to meet
Proofs of his rapine: but his wary fraud
Had baffled all their projects. Now his reign
Is cloſed. Hard preſs'd he drops the deer: the bait
His foes retards not; on himſelf they pour
Their utmoſt ſpeed. Falls his o'erlabour'd horſe
Headlong; uninjured from its back he ſprings,
And plies his nimble feet, and hopes eſcape.
In vain: the foreſt ſhakes him from its woods

Indignant,

Indignant, and its murder'd habitants
Avenges. With ſtrong gripe the keepers end
His fruitleſs ſtruggles; while the baying hounds
Leap round him, and with rage and conqueſt fluſh'd,
Scarce from his trembling limbs their fangs refrain.

WALK THE FOURTH.

AUTUMN.

Bright gleams the ray of morn; the gentle froſt
Has gemm'd with icy dew the graſs; in air
Floats the thin rhime diffuſed, not as when denſe
With wintry vapour its impervious fog
Blots out the neighbouring coverts, and each twig
Thickens with feathery ſilver, and the locks
Of peaſant loſt amidſt the dazzling gloom;
But twinkling in the ſunbeam ſpreads its veil,
Softening each harder outline, and apace
Before the aſcending radiance melts away.
Where in the hollow footſteps of the herd
Stagnate the reliques of the ſhower, with white
Network and cryſtal ſhoots the ſurface ſhines.
Lo! on yon branch, whoſe naked ſpray o'ertops
The oak's ſtill cluſtering ſhade, the fieldfares ſit
Torpid and motionleſs, yet peering round

Suspicious of deceit; at our approach
They mount, and loudly chattering from on high,
Bid the wild woods of human guile beware.

How richly varied is the scene! In vain
Spring with her emerald verdure, and the tints
Of bloom from every tree and bush and herb
Scattering its odours; with maturer greens,
Thickets with woodbine canopied, and banks
Ardent with blossom'd furze in gold array'd,
Summer in vain would emulate the charms
Of waning Autumn. What though one short night
Of premature severity, one blast
Whirling the fleecy hail, would strip the boughs,
As pestilence the crowded city thins?
What though already on yon windy brow
The lime and ash with unresisting fear
Their station have deserted? Unsubdued
Rises the mighty forest, and displays
Its splendid files. Seize we the present hour,
And view the fleeting glories ere they fade.
Mark the nice harmony which blends the whole
In one congenial mass, brilliant, yet chaste,
With every die that stains the withering leaf
Glowing, yet not discordant. Hither come,

Ye fons of imitative art *, who hang
The fictions of your pencils on our walls,
And call them landfcapes; where incongruous hues
Seem their conftrain'd vicinity to mourn,
Where gaudy green with gaudy yellow vies,
And blues and reds with adverfe afpect glare.
Here deign to learn from nature. Hither come,
Ye fons of imitative art, who fpot
With unconnected and unnumber'd lights
Your motley canvas; where the eye in vain
Seeks for a refting-place, and vainly ftrives
To trace the marr'd defign, midft dazzling fpecks
And univerfal glitter undefcried.
Here deign to learn from nature: here, though late,
Learn the peculiar majefty which crowns
The foreft, when the flowly paffing clouds
Triple † preponderance of fhadow fpread,

---

* The following lines refer only to the works of fome particular painters, and are by no means intended to convey indifcriminate cenfure.

† The painters moft fkilled in the management of light generally allow not above one quarter of the picture for the lights, including in this portion both the principal and fecondary lights; another quarter is as dark as poffible; the remaining half in middle tint. Sir Jofhua Reynolds's Notes on Mr. Mafon's Tranflation of Dufrefnoy's Art of Painting, p. 98.

And

And separate * the broad collected lights
With corresponding gloom; whether, beneath
These oaks that crowd the darken'd foreground seen,
Shine the illumined lawn and pasturing deer;
Or yon recess admits the fronting ray
Between its dusky barriers; or long gleams,
Stretch'd o'er the tufted surface of the woods,
Deepen the blackness of contiguous shade.

Nature, in all her works harmonious, blends
Extremes with soft gradation, and with tints
Kindred throughout her changeful robe adorns.
Bounds yon unbroken wood the level plain?
Light groupes detach'd and solitary trees
Unite them. Weave yon bushes o'er the hill
Uninterrupted thickets? Furzy brakes

* In the grouping of lights there should be a superiority of one over the rest; they should be separated, and varied in their shapes; there should not be less than three lights. The secondary lights ought, for the sake of harmony and union, to be of nearly equal brightness, though not of equal magnitude, with the principal. Sir J. Reynolds's Notes on Dufresnoy, p. 96. Yet neither any one of these secondary lights, nor all of them together, must come into any degree of competition with the principal mass of light. Sir J. Reynolds's Seven Discourses, p. 106. The highest finishing is labour in vain, unless at the same time there be preserved a breadth of light and shadow—the slightest sketch, where this breadth is preserved, will have effect. Notes on Dufresnoy, p. 99.

Aspire

Aspire to meet them. Spreads the furzy brake?
With varying breadth the intruding greensward winds,
And the rude mass with smoother maze divides.
And lo, even now when with autumnal gold
She decks the lofty branches, on each twig
Of humbler growth the many-colour'd fruit
Mindful she hangs. With ruddy clusters bends
The thorn: with brighter scarlet glows the brier:
Scarce can the sloe sustain its purple load,
Not yet from taste austere by frost matured;
While from the prickly shoots pale bryony,
Twined round the oft encircled stem, suspends
Its gorgeous berries: rich in glossy balls,
Privet's dark spikes with trembling lustre gleam.
Nor less the ground its hues accordant joins,
With faded leaves bestrewn, and floating wings
Of russet fern o'ershadow'd, whence upstarts
The woodcock; she who in Norwegian wastes,
Or Lapland's birchen forests, near the swamp
Suck'd from the muddy soil her prey, and nursed
Her progeny; till winter's rapid car,
On summer's steps close pressing, from his realms
Warn'd her, and earth her probing beak repell'd.

   Why in fix'd attitude beneath yon oak

Listen

Listen the deer? From morn to eve they stand
Expectant of the falling acorn. Hark!
From the bare bank it leaps. Quick to the sound
At once they turn, and seize it; then resume
Their posture. High above, the golden wren *
Sports on the boughs; she who her slender size
Vaunting, and radiant crest, half dares to vie
With those gay wanderers †, whose resplendent wings
With insect hum still flutter o'er the pride
Of Indian gardens, while the hollow tongue
Explores the flower, and drains the honied juice.

Now the chill'd evenings and the near approach
Of winter from the anxious cottage draw
You groupe in search of fuel. Youthful hands

* The golden crested wren is the least of British birds. It may readily be distinguished not only by its size, but by the beautiful scarlet mark on the head, bounded on each side by a fine yellow line—it frequents woods, and is found principally on oak trees. Though so small a bird, it endures our winters. Pennant's British Zoology, vol. i. p. 379, 380.

† "Humming-birds subsist on the nectar or sweet juice of flowers—they never settle on a flower during the action of extracting the juice; but flutter continually like bees, moving their wings very quick, and making a humming noise, whence their name." Latham's Synopsis of Birds, p. 770. "The above account of the manners will in general suit all the birds of this genus." Ibid. p. 771. On the structure of the tongue of the humming-bird, see ibid. p. 745.

Gather the scatter'd sticks, or with light hook
Fix'd to a pole pluck down the mouldering bough;
While the dead stump the sturdy peasant hews,
Or looking watchful round lest prying eyes
Observe him, from the oak by tempests torn
Rends off the shiver'd ruin with its load
Of leafy spray; backward he throws his weight,
And tugs with iron grasp; in vain the branch
Recoils with spring elastic, and in vain
Still by tough splinters to the trunk adheres.
Meantime yon boy in wanton mischief tears
The ivy twisted in contortions rude
Round the tall maple, and the stem divides
With stroke malicious. Soon the verdant mass,
Robb'd of its nutriment, shall fade, and while
The lifeless tendrils still their hold maintain,
To May's bright greens a dusky foil oppose.

How forcible the contrast, now the sun
Gilds the steep woods of these autumnal banks,
While an unvaried breadth of sober gloom
Purples the expanse below; where oft the heron,
Posted in Dove's rich meads, with patient guile
And pale gray plumes with watry blue suffused
Stands like a shadow; then with outstretch'd neck

Rises aloft, and to the distant fen,
Screaming, with solemn flappings wings her flight.
Thence Northward to those misty heights the eye
Glances, between whose craggy sides confined,
Low in his native dale, with stream as pure
As melts from mountain snows Dove laves his rocks
Wild as by magic planted, yet with grace *
Of symmetry arranged; now foaming darts
Along the stony channel, tufted isles
Now circles, now with glassy surface calm
Reflects th' impending glories of his hills.
Or turn we Southward, where on yonder cliff
High o'er his ampler wave projecting shine
Those ivy-mantled towers †; towers once with sighs
Sadden'd of captive Mary, jocund once

* "From the description given of Dovedale, even by men of taste, we had "conceived it to be a scene rather of curiosity than of beauty. We supposed "the rocks were formed into the most fantastic shapes; and expected to see a "gigantic display of all the conic sections. But we were agreeably deceived. "The whole composition is chaste, and picturesquely beautiful, in a high de- "gree." Mr. Gilpin's Observations on the Mountains and Lakes of Cumberland, &c. vol. ii. p. 228.

† Tutbury Castle, once the prison of Mary Queen of Scots; and in earlier times the residence of John of Gaunt.

With minſtrelſy, when Lancaſter conven'd
The throng of barons in his feſtive hall.
She knew no liberty, th' impriſon'd Queen,
Till death her chains unlooſed; with anguiſh faint
If ever the freſh gale ſhe ſought to breathe,
Frown'd the bleak battlement and guarded wall,
And mark'd her limits. Happier he, the bard,
Rov'd unreſtrain'd; and when his potent lord
Bade him the ſong prepare, theſe ſylvan depths,
Theſe ſilent glades inſtant he pierced, and hung
Even on yon oak his harp; then muſing ſtray'd;
Then vocal tried the meditated lay,
And ſwept the ſtrings; while gazed the liſtening deer,
And the woods rang with harmony divine.

Man loves the foreſt. Since in Eden's groves
His ſire, yet innocent, enraptur'd view'd
" Inſuperable height of loftieſt ſhade *,
" Cedar, and pine, and fir, and branching palm,
" A ſylvan ſcene," man has the foreſt lov'd.
Thoſe groves no autumn knew; eternal ſpring
With all the bleſſings of the varied year
In rich profuſion crown'd them. But when death

---

* Milton's Paradiſe Loſt, book iv. line 138—140.

Seized on his prey, fall'n man, deſtruction ſtretch'd
Acroſs the woods her ſceptre. With the axe
She fells them; with the tempeſt by the roots
Uptears them; by the waſting ſcythe of time
She lays them low; and yearly o'er their boughs
Still gay with life a robe funereal flings.
Yet ſhall eternal ſpring her ſway reſume
In that new promiſed earth, promiſed by voice
Of power unbounded and unfailing truth;
Where by no ſin to deſolation doom'd,
(For ſin ſhall not be there,) no ſtorms annoy'd,
No violence ravag'd, no decay impair'd,
Thy works, great God, for ſuch thy will, ſhall ſtand
Firm through the ages of Eternity.

WALK THE FIFTH.

WINTER.——SNOW.

At length th' expected snows descend. The earth
Her axis thrice has circled since the blast
Grew keen, still veering eastward; and when shone
The firmament on high with cloudless light,
Incumbent on the gray horizon's verge
A settled gloom has hung. This morn, when first
O'er yon bank climb'd the sun, a fleecy shower
Tinging with thin-spread white the frozen brook,
The bareworn track, and close-depastured plain,
Accompanied his course: ere long he chafed
The congregated vapours; yet, while noon
Blaz'd forth refulgent, from some half-form'd cloud,
Whose filmy veil by careless eyes unseen
Dimm'd, yet scarce dimm'd, the azure vault of heaven,
Descending oft the solitary flake
Foretold the secret purpose of the skies.

Now mid-day warmth declines; denfe haze obfcures
The turbid atmofphere; the clouds advance,
Not as the vehicles of rain, difpofed
In feparate maffes, and of varying hue;
Not like the manfions of fruit-wafting hail,
Lurid and dark; nor thofe where thunder dwells,
Of wildeft forms, fcowling with purple dies,
And 'gainft the nether ftreams of air propell'd
By their own currents; but of afpect dun,
Of texture uniform, and blending quick
In one unbroken furface, onward move
In firm array, and load the rifing gale.
Acrofs the whole ethereal arch they ftretch
Their dufky mantle; and while louder founds
And louder ftill the wind's tumultuous voice,
Now paufing, now with long and hollow fwell
Redoubling fierce, their arrowy ftores difcharge.

 While thus the echoing tempeft beats abroad,
Beneath th' impervious covert of this wood
Of antient hollies, whofe umbrageous heads
The gufts of Autumn have in vain affail'd,
Range we fecure, and view the diftant fcene.

 Mark on that road, whofe unobftructed courfe
With long white line th' unburied furze divides,

Yon

Yon solitary horseman urge his way.
He, not unmindful of the brooding storm,
Ere yet by strong necessity compell'd
Of pressing occupation he exchanged
The blazing hearth, the firm-compacted roof,
For naked forests and uncertain skies,
With wise precaution arm'd himself to meet
The winter's utmost rage. In silken folds
Twice round his neck the handkerchief he twin'd.
His legs he cased in boots of mighty size,
And oft experienced strength; warm'd through and through
In chimney-corner; and with glossy face
Prepar'd descending torrents to repel,
As roll the round drops from the silvery leaf
Of rain-besprinkled colewort, or the plumes
Of seagull sporting in the broken wave.
Then o'er his limbs the stout great-coat he drew,
With collar raised aloft, and threefold cape
Sweep below sweep in wide concentric curves
Low down his back dependent; on his breast
The folds he cross'd, and in its destin'd hole
Each straining button fix'd; erect he stood,
Like huge portmanteau on its end uprear'd.
Fearless he sallied forth; nor yet disdain'd

The

The heart'ning draught from tankard capp'd with foam,
By hoſt officious to the horſeblock borne
With ſteady hand, and eloquently prais'd;
While lingering on the ſtep his eye he turn'd
To every wind, and mark'd th' embattled clouds
Ranging their ſquadrons in the ſullen Eaſt.
How fares he now? Caught on the middle waſte,
Where no deep wood its hoſpitable gloom
Extends; no friendly thicket bids him cower
Beneath its tangled roof; no lonely tree
Prompts him to ſeek its leeward ſide; and cleave,
Erect and into narroweſt ſpace compreſt,
To the bare trunk, if haply it may ward
The driving tempeſt; with bewilder'd haſte
Onward he comes. " Hither direct thy ſpeed;
" This ſheltering wood —." He hears not! Mark his head
Oblique, preſented to the ſtorm; his hand,
Envelop'd deep beneath th' inverted cuff,
With ineffectual graſp ſtrives to confine
His ever flapping hat; the cold drench'd glove
Clings round th' impriſon'd fingers. O'er his knees
His coat's broad ſkirt, ſcanty now proved too late,
He pulls and pulls impatient, muttering wrath
At pilfering tailors. Baffled and perplex'd,

With

With joints benumb'd and aching, scarce he holds
The rein, scarce guides the steed with breathless toil
O'erpower'd, and shrinking sideways from the blast.
Mark how that steed, with icy mane, and head
Depressed, and quivering ears now forward bent,
Now backward swiftly thrown, and offering still
Their convex penthouse to the shifting gale;
Mark how that steed, on indurated balls
Of snow upraised, like schoolboy rear'd on stilts,
Labours unbalanced; the fallacious prop,
Now this, now that, breaks short; with sudden jerk
He sinks, half falling, and recovering quick
On legs of length unequal staggers along.
Trembles his rider; while the snow upheaves
In drifts athwart his course projected broad,
Or o'er the uncover'd gravel rattling sweeps
Caught up in sudden eddies, and aloft,
Like smoke, in suffocating volumes whirl'd.
The road he quits unwary, wandering wide
O'er the bleak waste, midst brushwood wrapt in snow,
Down rough declivities and fractured banks,
Through miry plashes, cavities unseen,
And bogs of treacherous surface; till afar
From all that meets his recollection borne,

Difmay'd by hazards fcarce efcaped, and dread
Of heavier perils imminent, he ftands
Difmounted, and aghaft. Now evening draws
Her gathering fhades around; the tempeft fierce
Drives fiercer. Chilled within him finks his heart,
Panting with quick vibrations. The wild blaft
Appall'd he hears, thinks on his wife and babes,
And doubts if ever he fhall fee them more.
But comfort is at hand; the fkies have fpent
In that laft guft their fury. From the weft
The fetting fun with horizontal gleam
Cleaves the denfe clouds; and through the golden breach
Strikes the fcathed oak, whofe branches peel'd and bare
'Gainft the retiring darknefs of the ftorm
With fiery radiance glow. The traveller views
The well-known landmark, lifts to heaven his eyes
Swimming with gratitude, the friendly track
Regains, and fpeeds exulting to his home.

WALK THE SIXTH.

WINTER.——FROST.

THE fleecy mantle which of late the lawns
Conceal'd, and burying deep the furzy brake
Display'd, upheaved in undulating mounds,
A rude resemblance of the forms below,
Is vanish'd. From the south dissolving gales
Blew; the snows felt their influence. In the woods,
Humid and comfortless, from dawn to eve
Were heard incessant drippings, pattering loud
When the wind moved the branches. The soft mass
Beneath of every drop the impression took,
Pierced into hollows numerous as the cells
That guard the luscious treasures of the bee.
Soon on the level plain green spots emerged,
Where raised the busy ant or delving mole
Its subterranean dwelling: floppy pools
In the surrounding pulp lay stagnant. Streams

Trickled from every bank; and down the hills
Spread sheety o'er the slopes, or rush'd amain
In the deep gullies. Swell'd the turbid brook,
And oft by congregated piles of ice
Obstructed, raged aloud, and strew'd the vale
With fragments. Of the universal white
No speck was left, save where in lonely dell,
Fronting the north, amidst the general rout
The drift its station still maintain'd, and seem'd
To wait for reinforcements from the skies.
Earth of its load was lighten'd, and absorb'd
The moisture: sunny gleams and breezy air
The surface dried. Now frost again ascends
His throne; and kindling with peculiar glow
Heaven's cloudless vault, and fixing firm the ground,
Crisp to the tread, from hot and crowded rooms
Calls us his bracing atmosphere to breathe,
And witness his invigorating power.

  Bend we our steps beside this forest brook,
And trace its windings. In yon flat morass,
Where spiry rushes in divergent files
Rise fledged with rhime, where many a stunted bush,
Alder or sallow, cropt by nibbling deer,
Betrays the dampness of the soil beneath,

From

From secret springs it rises. Issuing thence
Awhile in naked channel o'er the plain
It wanders; now in short and sudden turns
Twisting round narrow points, as though it fled
Back to its source; now in extended curves
Sweeping; now glistening in long reaches; now
With fretted surface and complaining sound
Hurrying down bright cascades. Thence swift it dives
Into this sylvan glen. Mark how it whirls
In circling eddies round that alder's root,
And far within the brink, where half congeal'd
Lingers the foam, the trout's dark hold prepares.
Here, the flat turf with easy flexure meets
The wave; abrupt with contrast bold descends
The adverse side, whence starts the aspiring ash,
Or time-worn maple, thorn, or sinewy oak
Deep-fix'd, and with its wreathed roots o'erhangs
The cavern'd margin. View the marly cliff,
Its base by oozing springs with frostwork glazed,
Various beyond the forms which fancy weaves;
Where crystal columns glitter, and disposed
Tier above tier, pellucid cornices,
With plumy darts and sparkling gems emboss'd,
Tell to what height the current lately raised

Its

Its ampler swell, and with diminish'd tide
Sunk gradual. Here, where in its pebbly bed
Rippling it runs, a narrow range of ice
Grows to the edge, or round the uncover'd stone
Concretes. There, where the broad and deeper reach
Spreads smooth, from bank to bank its pavement firm
Stretches, nor hides the gliding rill beneath:
Or by the stream deserted rears in air
Delusive bridges, to the heedless foot
Of deer, or stranger hasting o'er the wild,
Dangerous, and loudly crashing in their fall.
Lo! from its haunt, by crowding alders screen'd,
Where mantling in the still unfrozen flood
Aquatic weeds breathe warmth, at our approach
Alarm'd on sounding wings the wild duck soars,
And plies to distant solitudes her course.
The snipe flies screaming from the marshy verge,
And towers in airy circles o'er the wood,
Still heard at intervals; and oft returns,
Her favourite glade reluctant to forsake.

  Climb we this brow: the groves, whose naked
   scenes
Still have their charms, invite us. Mark yon oak,
Fix'd central in the opening lawn; while ranged
          Irregularly

Irregularly round to diſtance due
The ſubject woods retire. His rugged roots
Upheave the ſoil. His huge and furrow'd trunk,
Bulging with many a rough protuberance,
The lapſe atteſts of numerous ages, fled
With all their generations; while his top,
Pierced, and ſnapt ſhort, and deeply ſcorch'd, a blaſt
Wing'd with tempeſtuous lightning, and of more
Than common rage records. Projecting wide
O'er the bare plain with horizontal ſtretch,
His arms enormous, girt with wither'd leaves,
And tufted ſtill with miſleto, no more
By Druid hands and golden ſickle cropt,
Rear high their elbowy twiſtings; and uphold
With firm ſupport the thickly-woven ſpray.
Not ſo that lofty aſh, from yonder groupe
Advanced; the ſtem, patch'd with dark moſſes, lifts
Its flowing line; in light and wavy ſweeps
Diverge the branches, pendent, yet with points
Upturn'd, and ſable buds, loth to confide
Their winged foliage to the vernal breeze.
Cloſe by its ſide more pendent droops the birch,
With ſilver bark in flaky ſtripes detach'd
Conſpicuous, and in ſwelling veins prepares

Its vinous juice: behind, the dark yew frowns
With boughs elastic, once the bulwark deem'd
Of English freedom, when her warrior sons
Drew the long bow, and pointed shafts repell'd
Invading Gaul, or Caledonia's race.
With equal pride the clasping ivy boasts
Its leaf untamed; not as when, blotch'd by art,
With garish tints it decorates the wall
Of painted summer-house, or trim alcove;
But cloth'd in sober garb its tendrils flings
Amidst its native thickets; and in rough
And spiral coil wrapt round some neighbouring tree,
Hazle or maple, spreads its mantling robe,
And loads the boughs with verdure not their own.
But foremost of the band, whose hardy files
In summer vest the assaults of frost defy,
With glittering leaves and native coral shines
The holly: now its solitary cone
On pale gray trunk it raises; now combines
Its crowded tops and intermingling stems
In social groupes; now stretches o'er the hills
In woods continuous, with nocturnal gloom
Still dusky, save where through some narrow cleft
The searching ray finds entrance, or a shower

Of splendid atoms twinkles in the sun,
When from the rhimy boughs the ringdove breaks.
   Why gleams the axe? Why falls the verdant branch?
Falls it with emblematic green to deck
The fane, or in the cheerful window hung
The village grace; while man adoring learns
The wonders of his Saviour's birth, or hails
With festive gratitude the newborn year?
Still heavier found the unremitted blows,
And ampler desolation strews the ground.
Call'd by the well-known echoes, that bespeak
To all the herds throughout the neighbouring lawns
Scatter'd the hour of food, when sylvan spoils
The shrivel'd herbage of the plain supply,
Hasten in troops the deer. The prickly leaves
Fearless they crop; then seize the slender shoots;
Then from the firmer branches strip the rind,
Not doom'd, by schoolboy spread on viscous twig,
To snare the antient tenants of their shade.
Behind, the children of the hamlet throng
With cold stiff fingers, where the stagnant blood
Purples the skin, the abandon'd boughs to drag
Homewards. With fancy's eye I see them bend
At evening o'er the hearth, and watch the smoke

Burſt forth in puffs; while ſteams the bubbling ſap,
And hiſſes in the half-extinguiſh'd fire.

See in the vale, whoſe concave depth receives
The waters draining from theſe ſhelvy banks
When the ſhower beats, in ſlowly moving train
Penſive the cattle to the frozen pool
To quench their cuſtomary thirſt advance.
With wondering ſtare and fruitleſs ſearch they trace
The ſolid margin round. Awhile they ſtand
In diſappointment mute; with ponderous feet
Then bruiſe the ſurface: from the wood rebounds
Each ſtroke, forth guſhes the impriſon'd wave.

Thus through the ſylvan realms of Winter ſtray
Our devious ſteps. We linger, pleaſed to note
His mien peculiar. Deem we then the face
Of changeful ſeaſons varied but to charm
The gazing eye, and ſooth the vacant mind?
Say, is not nature's ample tome diſplay'd,
Even to the careleſs wanderer in the field,
With moral purpoſe? Wiſdom's dictates pure,
Truths of momentous import, character'd
By more than human finger, every page
Diſcloſes. He, who form'd this beauteous globe,
Studious amidſt its brighteſt ſcenes has hung

Fit

Fit emblems of a perishable world,
And all its transient glory. The full buds
Does spring unfold; and thick as drops of dew
Spangling the grass, the purple bloom diffuse?
Comes a chill blight, and bids the sanguine youth
Read in its ravages a lore that tells
Of frustrate plans, and disappointed hopes.
Do summer suns the mead with herbage load,
And tinge the ripening ear? With sudden rage
Descends the thunderstorm; the river swells
Impatient of control; and while its waves
Devour the promised harvest, calls aloud
On man to tremble for his daily bread.
The faded leaves does autumn scatter wide;
Or winter rend the desolated boughs,
And lay the fathers of the forest low?
The blast that executes their fierce command
To man proclaims, "This earth is not thy home."
It bids him seek, and heaven the search will bless,
A more enduring dwelling-place; the joys
Unutterable, which nor eye hath seen,
Nor ear hath heard, nor heart of man[*] conceived,

[*] 1 Cor. ii. 9.

Joys

Joys which Omnipotence itself prepares
For those who love their God; joys then to ope
Their stores, when the last trump shall shake the skies;
And all the palm-crown'd sons of holiness,
With garments wash'd in their Redeemer's blood*,
Shout their hosannas round his throne; and join'd
With angels, and to angels equal made,
Bathe in the fount of everlasting bliss.

* Rev. vii. 14.

FINIS.